TAKING L... ...
NOT TOO SERIOUSLY

a woman, a quirky mouse named Hugh,
and a life a half bubble off center
just like the rest of us

Stories and illustrations by
Maggie Clark

Write Way
Publishing Company
Print . Digital . Audio

Write Way Publishing
Company LLC

**Write Way Publishing
Company LLC**

Words for Maggie and Hugh Mouse

A wonderful collection of vignettes from Maggie and her alter ego, Hugh Mouse. They capture the laugh-out-loud humor in everyday life at home and out on the town.

— **Beth Bruno, author of *Wild Tulips***

Everyone needs a Hugh Mouse tale to brighten the day, lighten the spirit, and provide a whimsical point of view for dealing with life's little challenges.

— **Jean Partin, avid Hugh Mouse reader**

Author Maggie Clark has done a wonderful job of creating an alter ego character named Hugh Mouse. He is a sharp-tongued, witty, smart observer of human nature. A delightful read and a character you want to get to know.

— **Leigh Ballance, author of *The Secret of Gum Swamp***

Maggie Clark's Hugh Mouse stories offer both humor and sneaky truths about life. With her quick wit and twists peppered here and there, Clark has a relatable and charming character in Hugh.

— **Suzanne Crain Miller, author of *Queen*, *The Selections*, and *Wage***

A very special thank you goes to ...

- Lara Nowell for her story about the talking dogs
- Lynne Harris for her story about the waves in the toilet
- Leigh Balance for driving Miss Daisy around the golf course
- Jean Partin for trying to push toilet paper through her head
- My sister Becky Briscoe for her magic trick
- Jane and Gary Minor for their dream house on the river
- Jackie and Ralph McLean for trying to make a farmer out of me
- Ken Walmer for letting me ride his motorcycle
- The *Green Lake Reporter* for carrying my "Not Too Seriously" column
- The *Duplin Times* for pioneering their wheel and pulley technology in the 1950s
- My children, Fred Clark and Susan Head, for a bottomless well of subject matter
- My late husband, George, who said my mouse looked like me. What a guy.
- Diggy the mutt for being such a pain in the rump
- Cat Mojo for being, well, a cat
- Lee Heinrich at Write Way Publishing Company for her unceasing excitement and encouragement
- And last but not least, a big thank you to my friends, acquaintances, and readers who have encouraged me in this journey.

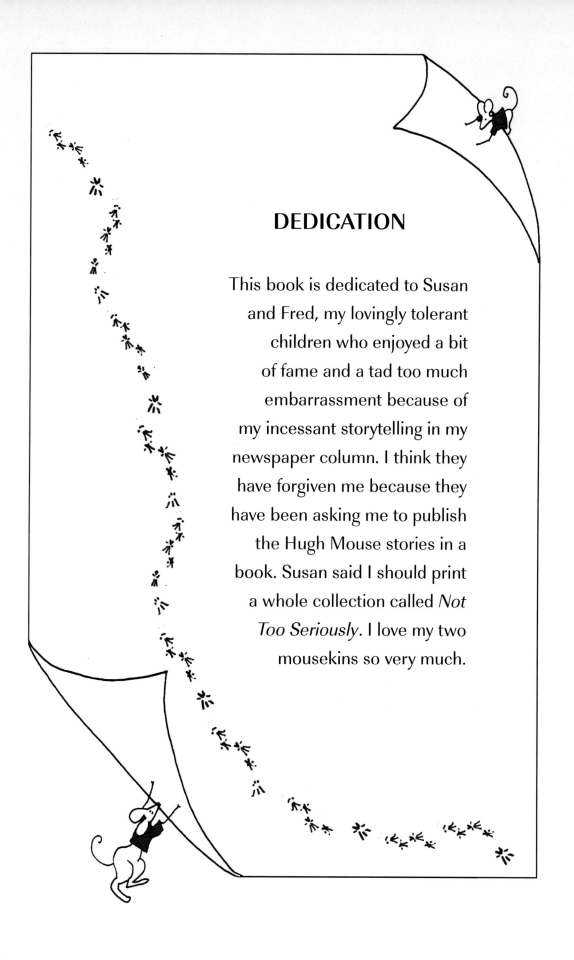

DEDICATION

This book is dedicated to Susan and Fred, my lovingly tolerant children who enjoyed a bit of fame and a tad too much embarrassment because of my incessant storytelling in my newspaper column. I think they have forgiven me because they have been asking me to publish the Hugh Mouse stories in a book. Susan said I should print a whole collection called *Not Too Seriously*. I love my two mousekins so very much.

TAKING

NOT TOO S

919-270-1666
Raleigh NC
hughmouse@att.net
http://HughMouseTellsStories.blogspot.com

or maybe sometimes foot in mouth ...

Slice-of-life stories told tongue in cheek ...

Author and illustrator of HUGH MOUSE TAILS

Maggie Clark

PREFACE

Who the heck is this Hugh Mouse character that frolics through the pages of my journal? Is he a figment of my imagination, or is he real? I just don't know. Sometimes I can't tell us apart.

This impish mouse was born in Wisconsin where I wrote a weekly column for the *Green Lake Reporter* called "Not Too Seriously." Just for fun, I drew a little mouse to illustrate it. My husband said, "That sassy critter looks just like you." He named him "Hugh." Go figure.

Speaking factually, Hugh is an inanimate line drawing. He's an explanatory device. He's a puff of smoke. But wait. You want the truth? He's a sarcastic little devil who has snuck into my journal. He watches over my shoulder as I write, and he even tries to grab the pen to give the story his own twist. He's just not normal.

My aim is to give you a few chuckles as you read these stories. They are meant to be silly and to be taken *NOT TOO SERIOUSLY.*

Dear Diary,

I'm Hugh Mouse, and I am living with a crazy family. What's wrong with them? Everybody knows that children watch cartoons in the living room on Saturday mornings. That's when Maggie and George get to have coffee in bed, read the paper, and laugh about the cute things the kids did that week. He brings her coffee, and she thanks him sweetly. Do I ever hear her thanking me for anything? Ha!

Why do Susan and Fred interrupt this utopia? Even the dog's there with his greedy paws on the bed, hoping someone will invite him up.

The newspapers get crumpled, coffee gets spilled, and the TV gets turned on so everybody can watch cartoons. Apparently, the tube TV in the bedroom has better cartoons than the HD TV in the living room.

Hey, is there no room for a cute little mousy like me?

No, this was NOT all right, Hugh, and yes, I DO mind if you write in my journal. Good grief, Mouse, is there no privacy around here?

"Happiness is having a large, loving, caring, close-knit family in another city."
— *George Burns*

3

Today I'm beginning my journal even though Hugh Mouse got hold of it first. It was clean and new before he wrote on the first page. I see he smudged it up a bit.

Why do I have this silly little mouse on my tail everywhere I go? Just last night I missed my turn because I was listening to him spin a yarn, and he was getting it all wrong. Can't somebody do something about this creature? He thinks he's human instead of imaginary!

Pssst! Over here. Maggie doesn't know it, but her kids like me a lot. Susan told me, "Hugh Mouse, you're pretty cool for a rodent." And Fred shares with me. Yesterday he whispered, "Hey, Hugh. Come to the kitchen, and I'll give you some cheese crackers. Mom told me to."

4

"Reality is merely an illusion, albeit a very persistent one."
— *Albert Einstein*

We left our friends' house late last night and made our way down their sloped driveway in spite of the ice and snow. I clung to George's arm desperately, hoping he could catch me if I started sliding. I was trying to be thoughtful. A guy needs to know his wife has confidence in him, right? We got to the car safely and after much—um, *discussion*, I guess you'd call it—George allowed me to be the designated driver.

We were parked on the right shoulder. I had to make a U-turn, so I was happy to see that the shoulder we were parked on was broad, offering me a wide arc to turn. I started the car and turned slightly to the right in anticipation of swinging around to the left for the U-turn. Being new to Wisconsin, it didn't occur to me that a ditch could be full of snow and look like flat ground. You guessed it.

The tow truck got us out easily, and the car wasn't damaged. George sat beside me, fuming. I could tell he was working really hard on self-control during the ride home because he was so quiet. He was doing a good job of it, too. I'm not his favorite driver, you see.

"God gave us a sense of humor because He took one look at what He had created and said, 'This is going to be pretty stressful.'"
— *Unknown*

I pulled into our driveway slowly, but the ice on it was thick and slick. The car started sliding. I was pumping the brakes carefully, as I had been told to do, until George shouted, "No, don't do that!" I immediately slammed on the brakes. I don't know if I did that because he startled me or because my foot didn't know what else to do.

As we slid closer and closer to the door, I started hitting the garage door opener like a crazed person. I prayed that I could aim the car through the opening. George, bless his heart, was stomping the floor with his foot like he was going to stop the car that way. I was willing that garage door to please, please, please go up faster!

Guess what I did to save the day? I honked the horn. The door must have heard it because it finally opened, and we slid right in.

Sometimes I think Maggie's a few bricks short of the whole nine yards.

"I base my reasoning on a stone which the builders of error have rejected."

— *Phineas Parkhurst Quimby*

Christmas is over, and I need to lose a little weight. But exercising is SO boring. They say you should warm up before working out. Shoot! If I do that, I'll be finished exercising. And then after exercise, you're supposed to slow down and stretch. Come on! Really?

Just to prove that I am an exercise optimist, I bought a "Long Length Tube," which is the politically correct name for "Lord, have mercy!" I put it under my feet and pulled the ends above my head. After I turned into a slingshot, I read the instructions. You're supposed to put it under your *arches*, not your *toes*. Hey, a monster rubber band isn't something you see every day.

I might be able to rig this thing up so that I can shoot cheese balls at Hugh. No, wait! That won't work. I keep forgetting he's me.

"Ability is what you're capable of doing. Motivation determines what you do. Attitude determines how well you do it."

— *Lou Holtz*

Today I saw Mojo sitting under the bedroom window, sort of hanging out, thinking he was being cool. But I knew what was really going on in his cat brain. He was wondering whether or not to jump up onto the window sill. The blinds were up, but was the window open? He couldn't tell. I knew it was closed – I mean it's *January in Wisconsin* after all–so I shooed him away.

I started to leave but I heard a thud. I turned around and saw saliva on the window glass and Mojo on the floor. I was worried that he might have broken his nose, but he sneezed a couple of times and started bathing himself as cats do when they don't know what else to do. Then he looked up at me as if to say, "So what are you looking at, Dimwit?"

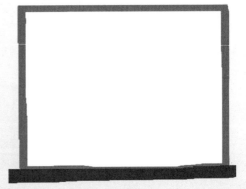

I left him still sitting on the floor looking at the window, tail twitching. I think he is plotting his revenge – because, of course, he's sure I did this to him intentionally.

It has been said by somebody that "A good laugh is sunshine in the house." Probably not so much today.

— *Unknown*

Mojo wasn't in the mood for a cat-and-mouse chase today (not that I'm complaining) because he was preoccupied with figuring out whether or not the window was open. Mojo isn't the brightest bulb on the Christmas tree. I knew the window was closed, but did I warn him? What do you think?

Hugh Mouse reporting here. Now I'm going to give you "the rest of the story."

Now get this picture. Maggie heard the Mojo thud, turned around, and saw the nose print on the window. She took a good look at Mojo shaking his head a little, and then I swear she laughed right in his haughty little cat face. Mojo could have broken his nose and she was strangling with giggles! I hope she feels awful about that on general animal principles.

Anyway, like she said, Cat Mojo gave her the evil eye before she left. He's still sitting on the floor looking at the window. But I know Mojo. His body language and twitching tail say he's plotting sweet revenge. I'm guessing something of Maggie's is going to get shredded in the not-too-distant future. Being a doofus, Mojo probably does think she did this to him on purpose. Cats!

I wrote my story, and Hugh came along and re-wrote it. Whose story is the best? You be the judge.

"Pain is life—the sharper, the more evidence of life."
— *Charles Lamb*

9

My washing machine has a "Casual" cycle. I don't know what's so casual about doing laundry. Can a machine agitate clothes casually? Maybe it's for washing clothes when I'm feeling casual about it. Maybe the washing machine wants to be used on "casual day" at the office. I'm going to write a letter:

Dear Kenmore,

I am applying for a job as a washing machine. Can you program me to relax when the "Casual" button is pushed? Can I get a setting for "Slow Down"? And I especially want to be programmed for automatic shut-off when the cycle is over.

I am willing to relocate. My preference is to be in a calm household.

Casually yours,

Maggie the Washerwoman

"How faded should these jeans be if they are to look properly casual?"
— *J. Ellsworth Kalas*

I was on the phone today after church. Since it's impossible for me to hold still, I was pacing and fidgeting. When my eyes strayed down to my feet, I did a double-take. What was that white thing at the bottom of my black slacks? I bent down and looked closer. Was it white fabric? It was inside my pant leg, hanging out. I tugged on it, and it kept coming out. What in the world?

Lo and behold, it was a handkerchief. (Yes, I use those old-fashioned linen things because tissues left in pockets snow on my laundry.) I guess it got stuck inside the pants when I laundered them.

Then I thought again. I was at church in those pants. Oh my goodness! Was that white handkerchief hanging out of my pants all morning? I don't even want to imagine what my friends thought! But then, are people really your friends if they don't tell you that you have spinach between your teeth or a white handkerchief hanging out of your pants?

Geez! The least my good buddy Hugh Mouse could have done was to tell me about it. He's down there at floor level all the time. Unfortunately, I didn't take him to church today. Oh, I forgot. Hugh exists only in my mind. Well, I guess I didn't take *that* to church, either.

"For me, style is a state of mind and individuality."
— *Tiger Shroff*

Susan and her cheerleader friends are wearing those mini skirt uniforms to the bus stop. Too short, too sexy, too in-your-face for this mom anyway. It's sub-zero weather! They tell me they are supposed to wear the uniforms to school on the days the boys have a game. Something about school spirit, they claim. Hmmm. I'm not too old to remember that excuse.

One girl said—and I have to agree with her—that the boys should be forced to wear their basketball shorts on game days. It's only fair. They could shiver and turn blue just like the girls. And the girls could whistle at them in the hall.

I know there are older and wiser cheerleaders at that school. I saw them when I picked up Susan last week. They wore sweat pants under the required mini skirt uniforms.

I started to suggest that to Susan. But then I shut my mousetrap. Why start an argument with an adolescent? There's just no future in it.

"It's impossible to believe the sperm that created this child beat out 1,000,000 others."
— *Unknown*

12

You have to be out of your mind to attempt to bathe a full-grown cat unless you're that lady on TV who demonstrates towel and strait jacket tortures to get a cat that she has drugged to hold still for a bath.

I have a friend who throws her two cats into the tub together and shuts the door. She says it works.

My sister says she stopped bathing cats the day hers walked up a fiberglass tub wall.

No thanks. No cat bathing for me. I'm more afraid of the cat than Hugh Mouse is.

"Help me not to live in fear of possible dangers."
— *Stormie Omartian,* **A Book of Prayer**

I gave the kids a magic kit for Christmas. I didn't tell them this story though—for reasons about to become obvious.

When their Aunt Becky—my creative and sly sister—was about six years old, she showed her new magic trick to her four-year-old friend Jean. She balled up a little wad of paper and supposedly pushed it through her head. An in-one-ear-and-out-the-other trick. Of course the real trick is to have another little ball of paper hidden in your other hand.

Jean was greatly impressed! Dumbfounded, in fact. She just *had* to learn that trick. So when Becky left the room, she rolled up a little ball of paper, stuck it in her ear, and attempted to push it through her head. She kept working that paper deeper and deeper into her ear until she conceded defeat, and then, wouldn't you know, she couldn't get it out.

Becky returned and, after trying to rectify the problem, she told Jean not to worry because it would grow out. Believing everything Becky said, naturally, Jean believed that too.

When the earache began a few days later, Jean didn't tell her mom there was a wad of paper in her ear. She was afraid she'd get Becky in trouble. Well, maybe she was more concerned about her own behind than Becky's. (Hugh must have said that, not I.) Anyhow, it was not growing out. It got infected, and Becky got busted. Thus ended my sister's career as a magician.

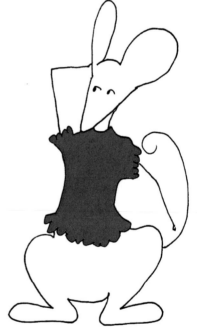

Jean says she learned two things that year. (1) Things are not always as they appear and (2) something embedded in a body part will never, ever grow out.

"Once you eliminate the impossible, whatever remains, no matter how improbable, must be the truth."   — *Sir Arthur Conan Doyle*

Yes, Cat Mojo is very mad at me. Just now he came and rubbed my leg. I went to the sofa, offered him some treats, and invited him to jump up on my lap for a little quality time. Instead, after consuming the treats, he turned his rear end toward me, jerked his tail in the air a few times, then sashayed to the window and sat down with his back to me. I think I've been mooned by a cat!

"You gotta love a cat, 'cause they sure ain't gonna love you."
— **George Clark Proverb**

15

Today my kids rigged up a wheel and pulley on the balcony for pulling toys and games upstairs. I laughed and told them my *Duplin Times* story.

It was the 1950s. At my dad's newspaper office, some creative person who was tired of running up and down the stairs had mounted a wheel and pulley on the upstairs ceiling, cut a hole in the floor below it, and attached clips to the rope so that they could send news stories up and down between the first and second floors. It was sort of a precursor to interoffice mail. I liked to clip rubber snakes onto it and send them down.

One day the guys downstairs sent up a real snake! It was a harmless little black snake, but I screamed so loudly that Dr. Gooding's nurse from the office building next door came running to check on us. That ended my mischief at the *Duplin Times*.

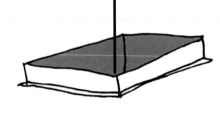

Oops! What have I done? My kids didn't really need this information. I'm sure a snake will be dangling in the hallway soon. I hope it's a rubber one.

16

"The best way to predict the future is to invent it."
— *Alan Ka*

GRITS

Cereal is good
  With honey and oats;
    While some folks like bacon
      With fried eggs and toast.

    Yet I've gotta say
      When a chilly day hits
      The breakfast that's best
      Is a bowl of hot grits.

    Just spoon up a serving
    Right out of the pot,
  Then add salt and butter,
    And serve piping hot.

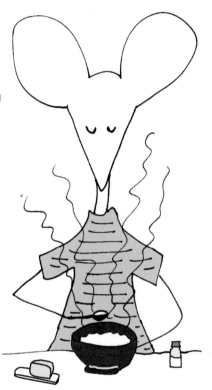

    Your fingers won't freeze
      When the frost is unkind
        If you'll just try to keep
          My suggestion in mind:

      When there's ice on the drive
        And it's snowing a blizzard,
        A bowlful of grits
          Will warm up your gizzard!

"YIPPEE! This taxi is off duty!" I silently cheered when my hubby offered to drive Susan to the movie. I told him he had to pick up two extra kids. Rule #1 in Taxi City: Children never go anywhere without bringing friends along.

He asked what time the movie started. 7:00. He asked what time he was to pick up the friends. I didn't know. He asked how long it would take to get to the movie via friends' houses. 39 minutes. Rule #2 in Taxi City: Mother's mental map and calculator must be available at all times.

He asked if I wanted to ride along. I bit my tongue and did not say, "Are you crazy?" Instead, I said, "No thanks. I have to wait for Fred's friend's mother's taxi service to bring him home." Also thinking, "Thank goodness it's her turn." Rule #3 in Taxi City: Never look a gift horse—er, gift taxi—in the mouth.

Hubby said he might shop for a lawn mower on his way home. Now I understood his generous offer to drive the taxi. Rule #4 in Taxi City: Surrogate taxi drivers get benefits as far as I'm concerned.

"You have to take what you can get when you're getting started."
— *Selena Quintanilla*

All I said at the dinner table was that liquor goes to your head faster if you drink on an empty stomach. Our teenage daughter remarked that it would do it even faster if you stood on your head.

The conversation turned to grade point averages. My husband said, "I'm sure it has to be high to get honors." Our daughter responded, "It ought to be! You put enough Tabasco on it!"

Our son, who was about as confused as I was, said (now pay attention, this gets complicated), "If someone is saying something sixty thousand miles an hour, and they don't make sense, you pick up your camera and tell them, 'I'm looking inside your head at your brain, and it looks like a double exposure.' "

This is a mystifying family.

"A person's speech hides his sanity."
— *Unknown*

The carpet cleaning guy came today. He walked in with a noisy vacuum and a big hose that snaked through the front door into the far reaches of the house. Cat Mojo was horrified and had to hide. He fled under the chair, and here came the big, bad man. Panic-stricken, he tore up the stairs. Here came the big, bad man again. Mojo whipped down the hall to the bedroom closet. And, yes, the big, bad man showed up again. Mojo hissed at the man, who laughed at him. This disturbed Mojo greatly.

Our stairway landing overlooks the living room, and on a good day Mojo likes to perch between the banister rails while he is watching the humans and hoping to spot Hugh Mouse. He never jumps off the landing. He's a smart cat.

Today, however, Mojo became Supercat. After exhausting all possibilities of escape upstairs, he catapulted to the staircase, hit the landing in one leap, soared between the rails at warp speed, never even touching the sofa below, and hit the floor running.

I'm sorry, Mojo, but humans have to clean carpets. You should know about these human things since you are the ruler of humankind in your cat mind.

"If everything seems under control, you're just not going fast enough."
— *Mario Andretti*

Egads! Am I turning into a mouse for real? Cheese keeps tasting better and better to me.

Having failed Memory 101 myself, I'm no good at teaching my ten-year-old son how to remember things. My parents used to say to me, "You'd forget your head if it wasn't attached," and now I'm telling him the same thing. In desperation I asked, "Fred, can you think of a trick for remembering things?"

He said, "Tying a string around your finger makes you look dumb. Instead, you should bite your finger." I said I'd never seen him walking around the house biting his finger. He said he does it at school. Really? Biting the finger is a creative idea, and saying he does it at school is a creative way to end the conversation.

"The advantage of a bad memory is that one enjoys several times the same good things for the first time."
— *Friedrich Nietzsche*

Today this city slicker sort of learned how to plant potatoes. While the kids were in school, my friends Jackie and Ralph took me out to Ralph's parents' farm to plant potatoes in his plot of ground. His whole family came to watch this.

My first lesson was that there is no such thing as a potato seed. Feeling a little dumb after that lesson, I tried to keep a low profile. The family was getting suspicious that Ralph himself might have become a city slicker. I guess that about put me in the category of a UFO.

I proceeded to watch the goings on in the field. Ralph and his sister disagreed on how to cut the potatoes. Then his brother told him how deep to plant them. Then his brother's wife, his other brother, his father, and his mother voiced some pretty convincing arguments about how and why the potatoes

should be cut a certain way, or not cut at all, and why they should be planted at this depth or that and at exactly what angle, and when to plant them. They must have been in agreement on that last one since everyone was present and accounted for.

You've probably guessed by now that Ralph planted the darn potatoes exactly the way he wanted to, and I kept a low profile. I am sure in years to come his family will be telling about the day the city slickers planted a garden.

"Farming looks mighty easy when your plow is a pencil and you're a thousand miles from the corn field."

— *Dwight D. Eisenhower*

23

George came out to the car to help me unload the concrete planter. He brought out our little four-wheel dolly. It's shaped sort of like a picture frame—you know, wood around the sides and nothing in the middle. It works fine for moving furniture, but I could see that the narrow base of the planter would fall through the doughnut hole. I found a large plastic container. We set it on the dolly upside down to create a tall platform. Then we slid the three-ton concrete planter onto it from the back of the car.

I started rolling this contraption across the driveway toward the garden. George said, "Watch that turn." I knew that. I rolled it around the garden hose slowly with a smirk on my face. What came next, he didn't warn me about because he could never have seen it coming. Not in a million years. As I rolled the dolly along the driveway, I started speeding up. My intention was to get up enough speed so that the dolly would keep rolling across the grass once it left the concrete. It didn't. I did.

In one nanosecond the dolly, the storage container, the three-ton concrete planter, and I blasted off. Most of me landed in the hole of the dolly with parts hanging off on the driveway and in the garden. After George pulled me up and saw that I was okay, he laughed his mouse tail off while I looked around the neighborhood to make sure no one else had seen this little mishap. To add insult to injury, he suggested I review Newton's law: "Things in motion tend to stay in motion." Well, I can tell you some do and some don't when they hit grass.

"Sometimes the only way you can feel good about yourself is by making someone else look bad. And I'm tired of making other people feel good about themselves."
— *Dan Castellaneta*

24

Cat Mojo was rubbing his paws across his ears again. I had postponed the inevitable as long as he or I could stand it. The time had come to do something. It took me one day to catch him and two days to catch and hold him. I squirted what I hoped was five drops of ear mite medicine into one ear before he rocketed away.

The third day I grabbed him in a clinch that a sumo wrestler couldn't have wriggled through. I apologized and cooed to him while reaching for the miticide. Forget about counting ear drops. I held him by the nape of his neck—and maybe a leg or two—and squirted at both ears.

On day four, I grabbed him and successfully treated both ears. He acted calmer that time. I should have known something was up. He was plotting.

On day five we stood in a face-down. His eyes said, "I've got the hang of it now, you idiot. Catch me if you can!" I lunged for him and could almost hear him chanting "Nanny-nanny-boo-boo" over his shoulder as he whizzed past.

Mojo might just get to keep his ear mites!

"I've had a wonderful time, but this wasn't it."

— *Groucho Marx*

Burned my darn finger again today even though I really was being careful this time. Honest. I used a potholder to pull the oven rack out to see if the pot pie was burning. See? Careful. My children think I *always* burn whatever is in our seldom-used oven.

The potholder slipped as I firmly took hold of the 400-degree oven rack. Or maybe it didn't slip. I think I thought it was protecting my whole hand and all its fingers. Paws. Claws. Whatever. Careful is as careful thinks he does.

The Bible promises me that one day I'll have a new body. That's a good thing. That includes a thumb.

"There is more stupidity than hydrogen in the universe, and it has a longer shelf life."
— *Frank Zappa*

The storm was awful! I was visiting my friend Lynne at the beach. Her house was high on stilts and, to my horror, it started rocking and rolling with the wind gusts. I didn't really want to know what that meant. I'm from the city. Houses have concrete foundations there. It was giving me the creeps that the house had started swaying. And swaying! And swaying!

Lynne saw my fear and tried to put me at ease. She laughed in a nice way—not smart-alecky like Hugh Mouse would have at something like this—and said,

"Where's your sense of humor?"

"Huh?"

She cocked her head and said with her little sideways grin, "Don't you think it's funny when you see waves in the toilet?"

I missed the humor. I just hoped there wouldn't be any breakers in there.

"I take a simple view of life. It is keep your eyes open and get on with it."
— *Laurence Sterne*

27

I got a new computer today. It made me remember our first computer. I had to call the child who sold it to us to ask how to turn it on. I thought, "Who needs this? My typewriter works just fine."

Then one day I decided I was going to master that monkey, and I was going to be patient about it. I had heard of a crazy woman who attacked her computer with a butcher knife. But I was cool. The computer was merely a tool and couldn't think for itself, although my son insisted that it could at least think better than I could. I told him, "Hey, wise guy, I betcha Hugh Mouse can out think you!"

I've gotten pretty good with computer stuff, but I still do think about that butcher knife sometimes.

It's about time Maggie joined the 21st century.

"With a furious man do not go, lest you learn his ways and set a snare for your soul."   — *Proverbs 22:24-25*

The hubby injured his wrist so guess who gets to cut his toenails? Good grief! Look at those claws! Somebody go find the buzz saw!

Why, oh why would you let your toenails get that long? Don't your shoes hurt? They do? So, you'd rather hurt than cut?

I watched him teeter on one foot with the toenail scissors in his hand and thought to myself, "He's going to break his neck if somebody doesn't intervene." I told him to sit on the floor and put a hand towel under his foot to catch the toenails that were going to fall on the carpet otherwise. I went and found better scissors. When I came back, he was sitting on the hand towel. I'm not sure how this happened. I visualized him inch-worming around the carpet chasing his toes.

A wave of pity consumed me. I sat on the floor, placed the towel under his feet again and started filing away at the big toe nail with an emery board. "Ouch!" he yelled.

I said, "I'm filing the top of the nail where it's jagged. I'm not touching any skin." I tried the larger nail clippers, but the nail was thicker than they were.

"Wait a minute," he said. He fetched some monster jaws of steel I had forgotten about. Very sharp. Very large. Very effective!

First clip – a nail shard flew across the room. I could forget about the hand towel. Get the shop vac. Half an hour later all ten nails were a tad shorter than before.

He's going to a nail salon next time.

29

My little mousekins saw their mom's true colors last week. They've known about my fly swat phobia from the git-go. I used to dare anyone to swat a fly on the table or smear one on the window or even brandish the filthy fly swat in my kitchen. I'd scream and spray disinfectant and wipe down all the counters.

Until one evening. I do not know what came over me. My daughter watched aghast as I jumped up from the sofa, ran into the kitchen, tore back to the living room with the fly swatter and smushed a fly on the lamp shade directly over her bowl of yogurt.

I was in the kitchen not long after when I wheeled around, grabbed the swatter, snuck up to the table, laid a lightning slap on a fly, and yelled, "Got him!"

My children are worried about me. So is Hugh.

Has she entered a higher realm of insanity?

"The Good Lord didn't create anything without a purpose. But flies come close."

— *Unknown*

30

My friend Jane told me that she and her husband, Gary, had planned a dream house beside a river, but they were in no hurry to build it. She laughed, "We'll be just fine as long as we can go to the river and fish and plant tomatoes."

I love it! She makes it sound so pleasant. There was a time when we almost built George's dream house. He dreamed of a house in the country, so we bought some land. I did not look forward to building on it because, well, let's just say we have different tastes in houses. But he wanted it. He said his dream house would have a rocking chair on the front porch. Give me a break! Even his boss asked him what he was going to do with a rocking chair. The man doesn't know how to relax.

Time passed, and we sold the land. We were at a party when the realtor called us. (It's one of those things that you remember where you were when you heard the news.) Yay! Have another glass of wine or two. I didn't want a house in the country in the first place.

George and I never did get that rocking chair on our porch or fish and tomatoes on our table. I think enough time has passed now that I'll tell him about my dream house at the beach.

"A house is made with walls and beams; a home is built with love and dreams." — *Ralph Waldo Emerson*

31

When you find out that raccoons carry a parasite that can make you go blind if the eggs get under your fingernails and find their way into your stomach, then getting children to clean under their nails suddenly takes on a new meaning.

Do parental warnings like, "You'll get worms!" have any effect?
Get serious.

Concerned parents might try bribery. But how do you set a price on a fingernail? A nickel a nail?

A parent might appeal to the child's sympathy: "What will people think of *me* if you have dirty fingernails?"

Also, there's the shock treatment, preceded with a gasp: *"Did your teacher see your hands today?"*

And there's humiliation: "Why don't you polish 'em pink, fella?"

After the child stares blankly at your noblest efforts, you might try violence. But does the crime really merit a flogging?

No. The only help at this point is a good strong dose of love and understanding. Administer gently three times a day. To the parent.

Hey, George. Maggie helped you with your toenails. The least you can do is help her with Fred's fingernails.

"Give me the communication, teaching, and nurturing skills that I must have."
— *Stormie Omartian,* **A Book of Prayer**

When Cat Mojo was in his prime, he could catch a fly in midair. Not so much now. When a moth fluttered by today, Mojo vaulted, but the moth got away easily.

Later, I saw the moth on the floor. Mojo saw it too. It jumped. Mojo jumped. The chase was on.

Mojo did his best to pounce on the poor moth. He jumped around in circles, hugging the floor after each leap, ready to spring again. He leaped but somehow the moth had disappeared.

Mojo held his crouched position, his body motionless while his head darted this way and that in search of his prey. Baffled, he finally stood up. Under him lay a flat, dead, not-so-interesting-anymore moth. He ate it nevertheless.

"Some people say that cats are sneaky, evil, and cruel. True, and they have many other fine qualities as well." — *Missy Dizick*

33

POTATO CHIPS AND ONION DIP

Oh give me nothing more in life
Than one small heavenly delight
To scoop a salty, ruffled chip
Into a pint of onion dip.

Three times a day I would indulge
But I must battle with the bulge;
I really love potato chips
With yummy, creamy onion dip.

In public places I resist
Potato chips and onion dip;
The world would see a different me—
I do not nibble daintily.

But back at home my kitchen holds
The goods, and many tales untold
Of gobbling up potato chips
And lots and lots of onion dip.

I try to stop. I really do.
But just one chip will lead to two;
A body needs a lot of chips
To tend a pint of onion dip.

When nauseously the stomach churns
(Though craving for them ever burns)
I have to force myself to quit
Devouring chips and onion dip.

Tomorrow will be certain death
With parched mouth and onion breath;
That's when I'll swear to never sin
And gorge myself like that again.

Yet what in life could ever beat
That yummy, tasty, salty treat,
That wondrous snack that makes me flip—
Potato chips and onion dip.

34

I was unprepared for the "Best Ball" tournament. They were unprepared for me, too, but never mind that. I was supposed to have brought my own group of four. The organizer had a little trouble finding a golf buddy for me. (I wonder why?)

Eventually, he found my good friend Leigh, who was there to watch his son-in-law and two grandsons play. Leigh got a third golf cart and said he would be "Driving Miss Daisy."

We drove to the first hole.
I panicked because I had forgotten to bring golf balls. (Give me a break! I only go to the driving range, and they provide the balls. I don't actually *play* golf!) Fortunately, Leigh had brought some extras.

I took out my driver and realized I had no tees. Leigh shook his head and said, "It takes a village." He gave me some tees and started asking me at every hole if I had a tee. He also kept a close eye on my clubs after retrieving my chipping wedge from the green.

On the last hole, my ball went into the sand trap beside the green. Leigh handed me the chipping wedge. Nobody bothered to take the flag pole out of the hole. They didn't expect me to hit the ball out of the sand, much less into the hole. But I nailed that sucker. It bounced twice, hit the flag pole, and dropped into the cup. I yelled, "Did you see that? Did you see that? Hey guys, did you see that?"

"I could've told you that, Tiger."

Leigh quietly said, "Yes, we saw that. Let's get out of here."

You don't yell on a golf course. You just don't.

"Don't go to the fishpond without a net."
— *Japanese Proverb*

35

I finished pulling the vines off the trellis this week. Geez. Those shoots were about to morph into "The Blob." Remember that scary movie? This vine was "The Blob with Tentacles." It had been probing around for something to grab, and I didn't want it to be me.

I started this project last week—by myself—with no help from anyone like maybe a husband. I stood on the tip-top of our rickety old four-foot ladder and pruned vine branches, even though Hugh Mouse said, "That's definitely a dumb idea." As I risked my neck, the thought passed through my head that maybe this dumb idea would draw some attention and possibly even some help,
but it didn't.

Yesterday I finished the job—by myself—on a nice sturdy aluminum ladder I had bought. George looked it over and told me that I should have bought a fiberglass one. I asked him when he planned to use it. That ended that conversation!

"You may not be interested in war, but war is interested in you."
— *Leon Trotsky*

This portable *#%$!! easel has finally drawn blood. It's a "French easel," and "*#%$!!" is probably mouse squeak for "French" or something. It's collapsible, and it doesn't discriminate upon whose thumb it collapses.

The process of setting up to paint usually includes a loud scream. Wood hits thumb or, even worse, hinge pinches fingers. Hence the missing skin not to mention the blood on this keyboard I'm typing on.

I bought Evil the Easel with good intentions, but our relationship is *over.* Now I'm bleeding while trying to eat my banana sandwich—just to prove I don't care—and searching online for a decent easel. Maybe one that's a lot kinder.

"Everything hurts."
— *Michelangelo*

37

Doggone it. Is this rascal Hugh Mouse really just a figment of my imagination? I keep feeding him chocolate, but it's never enough.

"I'd give up carbs, but I'm not a quitter."
— *Unknown*

Giving your daughter a home perm does not fall into the category of "joys of motherhood." Susan stayed motionless while I wrapped her up in a big garbage bag and tucked in paper towels here and there. She was waiting for me to lose my temper.

I parted her hair and tried to separate it into little squares, but that didn't work. I tried re-staking the territories, but that didn't work either. I gave up and put a curler in every hair swatch that seemed to be a different length. Grrrr, this was not fun.

As time passed, Susan's shoulders slumped more and more. I was almost crawling onto her shoulders to reach her head. Pretty soon I noticed that a lot of my hair clips were missing, and I snarled at her, "What are you doing with the hair clips?" I walked around to face her, and I saw hair clips decoratively lining the edges of her plastic "cape." I looked up, and she had clips on her lips and nose. We got the giggles, which turned into gales of laughter and tears. My husband looked in on us and decided everything was okay.

Later that night, Susan styled her hair, and I sat down to enjoy my Sunday night TV shows, but the ambiance was sort of messed up with the fragrance of a home perm lingering in the air. Not the most cheer-producing fragrance, but that's all right. Mothers aren't supposed to be cheerful all the time, but we can definitely kick into gear when needed.

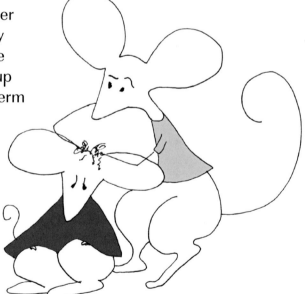

I am still steamed at my husband. He decided all by himself—no input from me—to adopt a dog. So now we have a dog. We were sitting at the dinner table one evening, and the stray dog that had been trying to adopt us was huddled up against the sliding door in the rain, putting on a "poor me" show with his big, sad eyes. George said with an air of finality, "Let him in." I glared at him.

Had I not made myself clear about that dog several times already? "Who's going to clean him up?" I asked. What a silly question. I bathed this smelly mutt. Somebody had to and every family member had magically disappeared. Even Hugh Mouse wasn't around to concoct his own story about this exercise in futility.

As I bathed the dog I thought, "This must be an old dog. Probably won't live but a year or two. There's a lot of gray hair on his face. He won't be around long." I was talking about the dog, not the husband, although the husband was slightly in danger at that point.

You don't neuter mice, do you?

The dog is still with us. The kids named him Digweed, but he doesn't dig. He rolls in stuff. (Try not to think about that.)

Diggy has never won my favor. He bites everyone who comes through the door. He got a surprise today though. In an attempt to calm him down, we had him neutered.

And that's about all I have to say about that subject.

40

"Now, now my good man, this is no time for making enemies."
— *Voltaire*

I was trying to talk my friend Ken into giving me a ride on his motorcycle today. He asked if I had a leather jacket. I asked, "Why do I need a leather jacket on a motorcycle?" There was dead silence. Apparently, anyone who didn't know that didn't deserve to ride on a motorcycle.

I volunteered, "I have a winter coat that is very warm. It has a fuzzy collar and everything."

He stared at me.

"What?" I asked.

He couldn't find words for it. He just said, "That won't work."

It took me a while, but I finally understood. He wouldn't be caught dead with a person with a fuzzy collar coat on his cool machine.

I guess I'll buy a leather jacket. I wonder if a pink one would be okay?

Just kidding.

"The single biggest problem of communication is the illusion that it has taken place." — *George Bernard Shaw*

My 13-year-old daughter can be a dingbat. I do not know where she gets it from. One morning this week, as I made her bag lunch, she walked through the kitchen asking, "Where is my shoe?"

"Shoe?" I asked. I looked down and, sure enough, she was wearing two socks and one shoe. I knew I would get a battery of insults if I suggested that it was probably within three feet of where she found the one she was wearing. So I tried to reword it, pointed at her foot, and asked, "Where was *that* shoe?"

She returned to her source, searched, reappeared, and said, "It's not there. Where is it?" I regretted having to tell her that the revelation had not come to me during her absence. But I did agree to make her toast while she continued searching.

As I buttered her toast, she arrived, fully shod and wearing *my* sweater. She asked—a little after the fact, it seemed to me—if she could wear it today, and I said "NO!" It was then that she flipped out. In the first place, I was mean and selfish. And in the second place, I hadn't done the laundry. And, third, I hadn't ironed her shirt from the last laundry day—a shirt that was really *my* shirt. She stormed back to her room fussing and slamming drawers. I could hear this from the kitchen. Then I heard her in my bedroom complaining loudly to her dad, "Mom hasn't done the laundry!"

I tried to stay cool, sat down to eat breakfast, and fantasized that my husband was properly defending me. Pretty soon, she entered the kitchen while buttoning a wrinkled shirt.

"I know that You have given her to me to care for and raise. Help me do that." — *Stormie Omartian*, **A Book of Prayer**

I asked, "Why don't you wear the clean sweater you wore last night?"

"It doesn't match these jeans! I would *never* wear that sweater with these jeans!" Dumb me. I must have been insane to suggest it.

The school bus came. I held the door open and watched Susan buzz through the house in search of her coat, then bolt out the door. I slammed it with a few choice words. My husband peeked around the corner looking perplexed. All I could say was, "She's thirteen."

I picked up the note she had left for me the day before. It was signed "Love, Suzi" with a big heart drawn around it.

My heart warmed, but I did not retract my Mother's Curse: "I hope you grow up and have a daughter just like your brother!" And there's a story for another day.

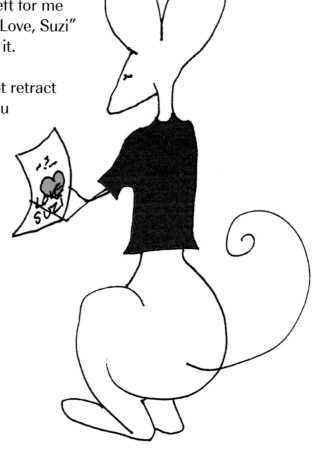

"Parenthood chooses you. And you open your eyes, look at what you've got, [and] say, 'Oh, my gosh.'" — *Marisa De Los Santos*

43

I opened the morning paper to find that
selfies with tigers are no longer legal.

Oh darn. I'll have to cancel my plans for today.

44

"There is a way that seems right to a man, but its end is
the way of death."   — Proverbs 16:25

November 19

I was visiting a friend when I heard strange noises outside. She laughed and walked me to the window. In her back yard, I saw her dog, whose name is Tux, and her neighbor's dog at the fence, and they were talking. Tux said, "Eoowwrrhh?" and the dog on the other side of the fence replied, "Oowowaawwwruh!" Then here came the neighbor. I watched as she picked up dog toys and old shoes. I looked at my friend with what I am sure was a befuddled expression.

Maybe dogs chew for fun, but I chew to make a clear path to something that smells good - like Gouda cheese!

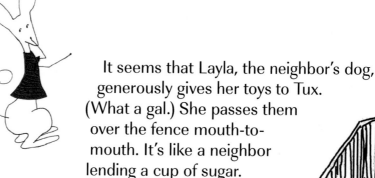

It seems that Layla, the neighbor's dog, generously gives her toys to Tux. (What a gal.) She passes them over the fence mouth-to-mouth. It's like a neighbor lending a cup of sugar. (Well, except for the mouth-to-mouth part. I guess that probably depends on the neighbor.) My friend's yard gradually fills up with Layla's ragged toys and chewed up shoes, then her neighbor retrieves them.

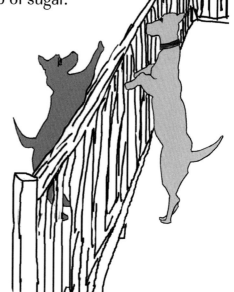

Layla is a smart dog. She has trained her owner to fetch.

"If we are eating only out of our own hand … we are in a downward path."
— *Oswald Chambers*

45

My brand spanking new printer decided to take ten and go on strike. It took me a while, but eventually I had to admit that I myself had caused the problem. Or possibly it was Hugh Mouse. Oh well, *somebody* had changed the paper size settings and the printer refused to pick up the wrong size paper. I'm sure I wouldn't do such a stupid thing. But somebody did. It turns out it's the printer that's the smart one here. And it looks like I'm the one that's—well—not so smart.

There should be a speaker somewhere on that printer that tells me what I'm doing wrong. No, wait. I've got a husband for that.

"It has become appallingly obvious that our technology has exceeded our humanity."
— *Albert Einstein*

Maggie isn't too happy about me writing in her diary, but I just can't help myself. Today was too good to leave unwritten.

Hugh Mouse, this is your last warning. Quit writing in my journal or pack your bags. Your choice.

"Oooo" and "Ah!" sounds drifted down the hall this afternoon. I wondered how Maggie was going to react. Susan and Fred were in her room playing with Susan's new chemistry set. They brought some green stuff to the kitchen. They had mixed some red stuff with some white stuff. To get green? They showed it to Maggie, and she laughed. So far so good.

They went back to their lab. Soon I heard "barf-face!" and Susan ran to the kitchen looking for two glasses and a straw. "You're not going to drink it!" Maggie gasped. Susan rolled her eyes, which always pleases her mom so much.
"No way, Mom! We're doing a color-blowing experiment." she said, scurrying away.

Time passed. Then I heard, "Oh no! Mom! We dropped something on the carpet and Diggy ate it!" I cringed. Maggie tore down the hall, and I came in a close second. Yep. There it was. A heaving dog and a pile of "green stuff" on the carpet.

Oh my goodness. The rest is history, and I'm telling you, this dog had better count his blessings while he still can!

"All of us have moments in our lives that test our courage. Taking children into a house with a white carpet is one of them."
— *Erma Bombeck*

December 9

"Mah-a-a-a-m-m!" When my children stretch "Mom" out to six syllables it means, "Mom, why are you doing this horrible thing to me?!" and when they find out I've written something about them in my newspaper column it means, "Mom, you are a beast and you have made me the laughingstock of the whole school!" You'd think I was Attila the Mom or something.

Uh oh. Hugh just showed up.

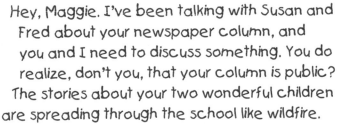

Hey, Maggie. I've been talking with Susan and Fred about your newspaper column, and you and I need to discuss something. You do realize, don't you, that your column is public? The stories about your two wonderful children are spreading through the school like wildfire. You've got to control your pen. Why don't you let me take over?

Ha! When the Amazon River freezes over! I like to write about new experiences, and people love to read a Southern transplant's viewpoint about things like deer hunting. It's such a big deal in this town that the stores close for firearms week during hunting season. Anyway, the little vignettes I write are all in fun.

That may be true, Attila, but an expository story is not appropriate when your 13-year-old daughter's friend asks her if she likes venison and Susan replies, "Who's that?"

"Denial is a common tactic that substitutes deliberate ignorance for thoughtful planning."
— *Charles Tremper*

I make cookies about once a decade. Today I was stirring some gooey, oatmeally, peanutty cookie dough. After I swooped the final pass around the bowl, the last glob of dough stayed stuck to the wooden spoon. With fingers that were "impeccably clean," as Julia Child would say, I pushed the dough down and off the wooden spoon. Or shall I say, I pushed *some* of the dough off. The spoon flipped and I slung a glob of cookie dough somewhere out into left field, and
that's how I invented the Cookie
Dough Catapult.

"I have not failed. I've just found 10,000 ways that won't work."
— *Thomas Alva Edison*

49

December 20

The wax Maggie melted tonight in her new electric candle wax melter has an apple cinnamon crisp scent that's to die for. The aroma has wafted down here into my cozy little mouse hole. That gadget works great because it's difficult for Maggie to burn the house down with it.

Dearest Diary, I see you've let Hugh Mouse write in my journal tonight. Thanks a lot!

Safe or not, I don't trust it. Maggie needs to turn it off at night. That means she has to remember that she turned it on in the first place. You think I shouldn't worry? Hey, this is Maggie I'm talking about.

When she turned on that gadget for the first time yesterday, I saw her turn on lamps and light switches in odd places around the house. Then I saw her put an unlit candle on her pillow. I was curious as heck so I stayed awake late last night to see if she had a plan or if this was a light bulb fetish I didn't know about. Here's what happened.

She yawned, turned off the TV, and headed for bed. What I feared most was happening. She was forgetting to turn off that electric wax melter and was putting her whole house—and me—in danger of burning up. But wait. Before the raging inferno could begin, she noticed that the light was on in the hall. She walked to that light switch and then noticed that the light was on in the dining room. She walked into the dining room and noticed that the light was on in the kitchen. She walked into the kitchen and turned off the

"Each problem that I solved became a rule which served afterwards to solve other problems."
— *René Descartes*

light switch. She started to leave but couldn't help but notice that the light on the range hood was on, so she walked over to the stove and—BINGO— she saw that the electric wax melter was still turned on. She had thought this through like nobody else could have thought it through.

You're now wondering about that unlit candle she had put on her pillow. Glad you asked. When Maggie got everything turned off, I tiptoed behind her into the bedroom. She picked up the candle from her pillow, set it on the bedside table, smiled, and said, "Got-'er done."

Apparently, the candle was her backup reminder that there was something in the house that was out of the ordinary, and it had something to do with a candle. Now I understand what Fred and Susan mean when they say, "It's a mom thing."

I have a new respect for this woman. In the future, whenever I need a little assistance with my memory, I'm going to ask Maggie to engineer something for me. She knows how to use the part of her brain that thinks backwards.

"Things yet unknown will change the way you think."
— *Toba Beta,* **Master of Stupidity**

December 26

The choir had rehearsed long and hard for the Cantata. I made a point to turn off my cell phone ringer. So glad I remembered that.

People started pouring in and the volume escalated. When the service began, quiet descended, and the silence was deafening. About ten seconds into the opening prayer, I heard someone's cell phone ring behind me, and—darndest thing—their ring tone was the same as mine. I spent a moment pondering that coincidence before it occurred to me that it *was* mine. I crouched down, as if no one would know I was there, scrambled through my purse for the phone, and then fumbled with it until I got the volume turned off. So easy to do when I'm not panicking.

After that humiliation, the choir began their holy music. I guess my phone was not turned off after all because my alarm started playing a tune. So, I sat on the phone. (Hey, that works in the car. Can't hear it at all.) As I sat there on the proverbial egg I had laid, I mentally rehearsed what I would do to turn everything off. Then I removed it from under my derriere, turned it off very quickly, and jammed it back into my purse. About five minutes later, my purse fell off the pew with a loud *thunk*.

The Bible says, "Judge not, lest ye be judged." I vow never again to be critical when someone's cell phone goes off in church.

"Whenever you get one inch above the ground in your own esteem, you are that inch too high!" — *Charles Spurgeon*

52

SAY GOODNIGHT, HUGH MOUSE

Truly I'm too tired to write.
I think I'll just turn in tonight.

I've had a week – as mothers do –
Of ear infections, fevers too.

A mall trip in the afternoon;
The squabbling started way too soon.

We ordered hot dogs after that,
They never came, and there we sat.

My aching feet got rested, then
A zoo trip made them hurt again.

Riding home was really great
Except for horns and rubber snakes.

Then chores at home made me uptight.
I'm beat. Hugh Mouse, just say goodnight!

53

About the Author

Maggie Clark is a humorist who started writing as soon as she could hold a pen. As a child, she tried to frustrate her first grade teacher into teaching her cursive, and she published many a book of pencil-written poems bound with a well-placed staple or two.

She grew up in a family newspaper business, the *Duplin Times*, in Kenansville, North Carolina, and wrote a weekly column for the paper during her high school years. As a newspaper columnist at the *Green Lake Reporter* in Wisconsin in 1985, she gained an enthusiastic audience for her vignettes about everyday life. After returning to the South, she continued writing her whimsical stories, even while working as a professional fine artist and later running a sign business with her husband in Raleigh, North Carolina.

For years folks have read Maggie's newspaper columns and blog posts and chuckled at her unexpected comments about life's missteps, often laughing, "That happened to me, too!" While Maggie admits that "stuff just happens" to her, she claims that her stories come from a little mouse who whispers in her ear.

In this book, Hugh Mouse watches from the sidelines (and occasionally sneaks in his own account of things) as Maggie candidly offers her observations to the reader through a peek at her journal.

Upcoming books in Maggie's *Not Too Seriously* series will give readers stories about painting, housekeeping, cats, dogs, care giving, grandparenting, relocating, traveling, golden years dating, and great grandpa's tales.

Dear Reader,

Thank you for reading my little stories. I hope you had as much fun reading them as I had writing them.

You can keep up with the latest Hugh Mouse activity on my new blog at NotTooSeriously.com. I hope you will drop by for a visit. After all, you never know what fun things Hugh Mouse might be up to just to make his readers happy! You know you can't keep that sneaky little guy from sticking in his two cents every now and then.

And if you are so inclined, Hugh and I would welcome and truly appreciate a review on our Amazon book page.

Maggie and  Hugh

Made in the USA
Lexington, KY
24 September 2017